POLICE OFFICERS
A First Look

PERCY LEED

GRL Consultant, Diane Craig, Certified Literacy Specialist

Lerner Publications ◆ Minneapolis

Educator Toolbox

Reading books is a great way for kids to express what they're interested in. Before reading this title, ask the reader these questions:

What do you think this book is about? Look at the cover for clues.

What do you already know about police officers?

What do you want to learn about police officers?

Let's Read Together

Encourage the reader to use the pictures to understand the text.

Point out when the reader successfully sounds out a word.

Praise the reader for recognizing sight words such as *to* and *that*.

TABLE OF CONTENTS

Police Officers 4

Police Officers

Police officers keep people and places safe.

The police make sure
people follow laws.

They help when people are lost or hurt.

The police work
in small towns.

They work in big cities too.

Do you live in a small town or big city?

Police cars have
bright lights.
They make loud
sounds.

Why do police cars make loud sounds?

badge

uniform

Police wear uniforms and badges.
These tell people that they are police.

Police dogs help find things.

Have you ever seen a police dog?

They can smell more things than people.

People must train to be police officers. They learn how to help people.

Police officers work together.

They work with the people they serve too.

Police officers work hard to keep people safe!

You Connect!

What is something you like about police officers?

What is something or someone that makes you feel safe?

Would you like to be a police officer when you grow up?

Social and Emotional Snapshot

Student voice is crucial to building reader confidence. Ask the reader:

What is your favorite part of this book?

What is something you learned from this book?

Did this book remind you of any community helpers you've met?

Photo Glossary

badge

police car

police dog

uniform

Learn More

McDonald, Amy. *Police Cars*. Minneapolis: Bellwether Media, 2022.

Schuh, Mari. *All about Police Officers*. Minneapolis: Lerner Publications, 2021.

Waxman, Laura Hamilton. *Police Officer Tools*. Minneapolis: Lerner Publications, 2020.

Index

Photo Acknowledgments

The images in this book are used with the permission of: © PeopleImages.com - Yuri A/Shutterstock Images, pp. 4–5; © rh2010/Adobe Stock, p. 6; © antoniodiaz/Shutterstock Images, p. 7; © RyanJLane/iStockphoto, p. 8; © carstenbrandt/iStockphoto, p. 9; © John M. Chase/iStockphoto, pp. 10–11, 23 (top right); © VAKSMANV/Adobe Stock, pp. 12–13, 23 (top left, bottom right); © Hakim Graphy/Shutterstock Images, pp. 14, 23 (bottom left); © Eric Weiner/Wikimedia Commons, p. 15; © fstop123/iStockphoto, pp. 16–17; © LightField Studios/Shutterstock Images, p. 18; © SDI Productions/iStockphoto, p. 19; © kali9/iStockphoto, p. 20.

Cover Photograph: © kali9/iStockphoto

Design Elements: © Mighty Media, Inc.

Lerner Publications Company
An imprint of Lerner Publishing Group, Inc.
241 First Avenue North
Minneapolis, MN 55401 USA

For reading levels and more information, look up this title at www.lernerbooks.com.

Main body text set in Mikado a Medium.
Typeface provided by Hannes von Doehren.

Library of Congress Cataloging-in-Publication Data

Names: Leed, Percy, 1968–author.
Title: Police officers : a first look / Percy Leed.
Description: Minneapolis, MN : Lerner Publications, [2025] | Series: Read about community helpers | Includes bibliographical references and index. | Audience: Ages 5–8 | Audience: Grades K–1 | Summary: "Police officers help keep our communities safe. Colorful photographs and leveled text allow readers to a peek into the daily work of these important community helpers"—Provided by publisher.
Identifiers: LCCN 2023035568 (print) | LCCN 2023035569 (ebook) | ISBN 9798765626450 (library binding) | ISBN 9798765629574 (paperback) | ISBN 9798765636961 (epub)
Subjects: LCSH: Police—Juvenile literature.
Classification: LCC HV7922 .L44 2025 (print) | LCC HV7922 (ebook) | DDC 363.2—dc23/eng/20231213

LC record available at https://lccn.loc.gov/2023035568
LC ebook record available at https://lccn.loc.gov/2023035569

Manufactured in the United States of America
1 – CG – 7/15/24